Clouds: Forecasting and Fun Trivia about Clouds for Kids

Copyright 2014 by:
Cody Miller

Cody Miller

Table of Contents

Gift For You 3
Look Up at the Sky 5
What are Clouds? 7
How Clouds Form 9
Types of Clouds 13
Types of Weather 19
Cloud Forecasting 25
Fun Facts 29
References 36
Gift For You 38

Gift For You

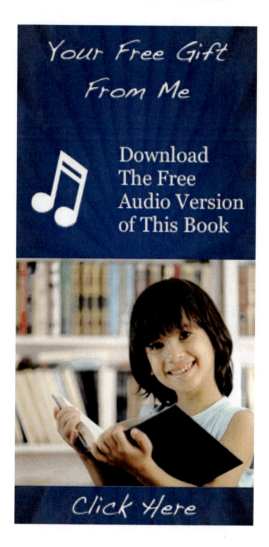

Go here for your gift:

http://freebiebonus.com/cloudaudiobookbonus

Cody Miller

Look Up at the Sky

Cumulus clouds in fair weather

Look up in the sky, what do you see? Unless it's a very clear day, you're sure to see at least a few clouds slowly moving across the sky. Most people see clouds nearly every day, but few know what they really are. Meteorologists and other scientists are fascinated by clouds because they can help predict weather conditions and explain other phenomena. Here are some fun facts about clouds.

Cody Miller

What are Clouds?

Every cloud is made from either liquid droplets or frozen crystals that have formed together into a semi-solid mass that is so light that it can float in the sky. The particles that make up the cloud are known as aerosols due to how they interact with the air and atmosphere.

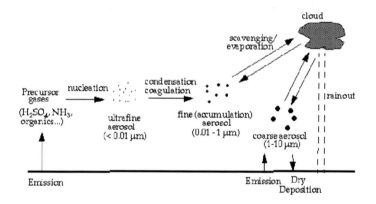

Even though nearly every cloud is made from water, they don't have to be. In fact, most clouds have other chemicals and particles trapped in them. A cloud can form entirely from chemicals or water-like substances, but these clouds are very uncommon.

There is a specific branch of meteorology dedicated to understanding how clouds move, known as cloud physics. This helps meteorologists understand where clouds will go and how storms both form and move.

This cloud is most likely known as altocumulus

How Clouds Form

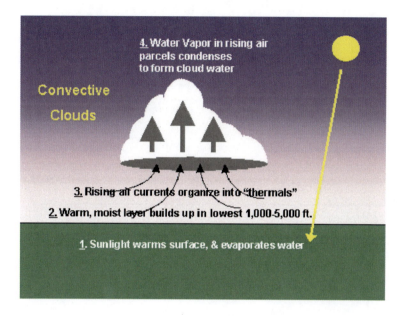

The sky is full of tiny droplets of water. However, you can't see or feel these droplets because they are too tiny and there isn't enough in a given space. But, when these droplets form into a vapor and collect in one area, it will form a cloud.

Cody Miller

Water vapor is caused by many things, but it most commonly happens when the sun causes a body of water to partially evaporate. The evaporated water turns into a vapor that rises into the air. As it rises, the vapor condenses and pulls together, but that's only part of how a cloud forms.

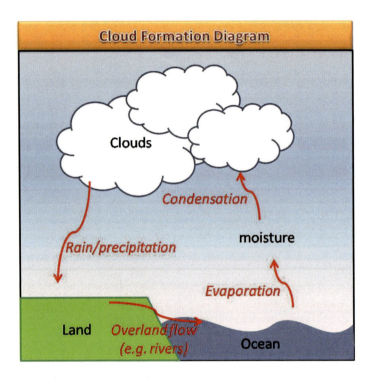

As the water vapor condenses, the droplets have to stick to something to stay in the air. Believe it or not, there is a lot of dust in our environment that's floating in the air. The droplets are able to stick to the dust and other particles in the air. Once there are billions of drops in one place, you will see a cloud.

If the drops cannot stick to a particle, then they will eventually fall back to the ground, but this might take a long time depending on the weather conditions.

Cody Miller

Types of Clouds

There are many different types of clouds, but the main ones are named for their position and shape.

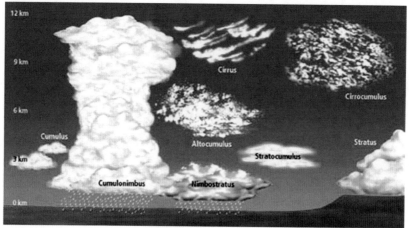

Types of clouds

Clouds have simple names based on their position. High clouds are small and very high in the atmosphere. Middle clouds are larger and closer to the ground. Low clouds are even closer to the ground. Fog is the result of very low clouds. The cloud touches the ground and makes it difficult to see through the water vapor.

Cody Miller

Cirrus clouds are curly and other look like feathers. They are high in the atmosphere, at least 20,000 feet above the ground, which makes them high clouds. These clouds are perpetually frozen due to how high they are. If you see these clouds, then an unsettled storm system might also appear within 12 to 18 hours, but there aren't always storms.

Stratus: These clouds are considered middle clouds because they are between high and short clouds and they are about 6,000 to 20,000 feet above the ground. Since these clouds are very thick, the sun can sometimes shine through them like a pane of frosted glass. They will look like a large, even sheet that's covering the sky. If they have enough precipitation, then stratus clouds often mean that a light rain (or snow, if it's winter) will occur within a few hours.

Cody Miller

Cumulus: The majority of cumulus clouds are low clouds that are up to 6,000 feet in the air. These are the large, lumpy clouds that you'll often see in the sky. These clouds tend to look the biggest because they are the closest to the ground.

Clouds: Shapes, Forecasting and Fun Trivia about Clouds

If you see cumulus clouds, then you'll probably experience fair weather since cumulus clouds aren't known for commonly having precipitation. However, these clouds can sometimes appear before a moderate to severe thunderstorm. Tornadoes may also form from these clouds, but the chance of this is incredibly low.

Cumulonimbus: These are cumulus clouds that are almost completely associated with thunderstorms and bad weather conditions. They are structurally the same as cumulus clouds (large and lumpy), but the major difference is that they are very high vertically in the sky. These clouds can reach up to 60,000 feet in the air, which gives them an anvil-like shape. If you see these clouds, then bad weather is coming.

Types of Weather

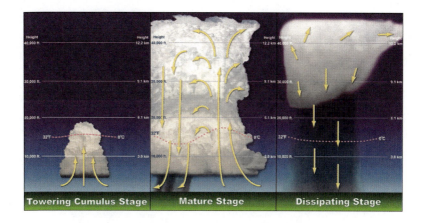

Clouds and weather are very closely associated because all of the Earth's rain comes from some type of cloud system. The air near the cloud has to be cooled to form rain, and this can happen in three different ways. The cooling method and various other factors can determine what type of rain system you have.

Cody Miller

Convectional Rain: This type of rain primarily occurs due to heat. Warm days will generate a lot of sunshine and heat. This will cause the ground to give off lots of warmth, which will soon hit the cloud. Since warm air rises, the cloud will gradually rise higher into the atmosphere. It will also gather more water since warm air can hold more water than cold air.

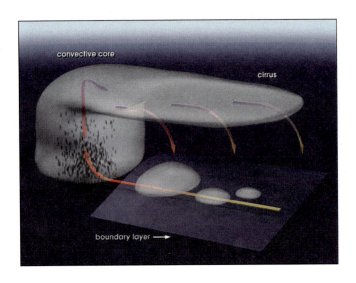

As the cloud gets higher, it will begin to get colder. When the cloud gets too high, and also too cold, the temperature will force the extra water to condense. This will cause very intense rain, and even lightning and thunder are possible. You will typically see these clouds on a very hot day. If it's incredibly hot, then these clouds can form and expel water within 10 minutes, but it typically takes one or several hours before convectional rain occurs.

Frontal Rain: This is very similar to convectional rain systems since it involves heat, but the storms aren't nearly as strong and there's much less heat involved in this type of rain system. Not only that, but this can occur on colder days since there's less heat. Two types of air will meet: a body of air that's relatively warm and another that's relatively cold.

The temperatures don't exactly matter, but they must be different enough to be considered warm and cold. The warm air isn't as dense, which causes the cold body to move higher into the atmosphere. This forces the colder mass to condense and become even cooler. When the cloud becomes too cold, it will rain. These rain systems typically involve large gray clouds that cover the majority of the sky.

Relief Rain: This occurs due to large physical obstructions, like mountains and large hills. A body of warm air will be moving as normal, but it will be forced into the atmosphere due to the obstruction pushing it upwards. This causes the air to cool and eventually cause rain. Unlike the other rain systems, the cloud will eventually drop back down because it isn't as cold as with the other rain systems.

Cody Miller

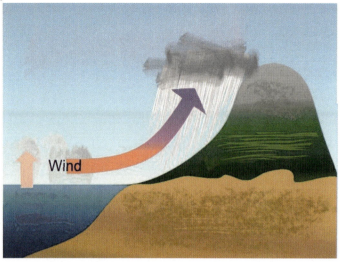

This leads to much drier air since the cloud has lost a lot of moisture. Relief rain is very unique because it's caused by the physical environment. For example, one side of a mountain might have lots of rain while another is relatively dry due to the mountain's formation.

Cloud Forecasting

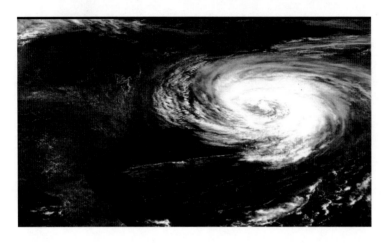

Even though it might seem archaic and it's subject to inaccuracies, you can use clouds to forecast the weather. In fact, meteorologists will use cloud shape, movement and formation to figure out how storm systems and weather conditions will develop. Even though they are using satellite images and years of experience to translate how the clouds are moving, you can do the same with a discerning eye.

Cody Miller

Warm Front: Warm fronts can lead to unstable storms and environmental conditions. You can predict a warm front by checking the clouds. There has to be a significant amount of cloud coverage that starts with cirrus clouds before turning into stratus ones. These systems typically have thunderstorms. If you see this type of cloud activity, then a storm will probably start within six to eight hours.

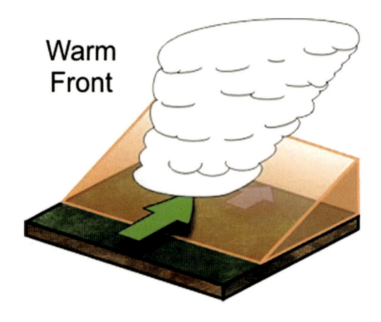

Clouds: Shapes, Forecasting and Fun Trivia about Clouds

Cold Front

Cold Front: Cold fronts typically aren't as bad from a storm perspective, but they can also form thunderstorms and harsh rains. You will typically see a lot of anvil cirrus clouds (the ones that reach high into the sky) and some stratus ones. This type of front is harder to predict because it moves faster, the cloud coverage is fairly thin and common to normal conditions and it might only be an hour or less before rain starts.

High-pressure Fronts: This usually indicates that the weather will be fair for the day. You will often see a mass of cumulus or cirrus clouds that don't move very quickly or change often. Humidity might be an issue on warmer days, but this is typically a good type of system to see because high pressure often leads to good weather.

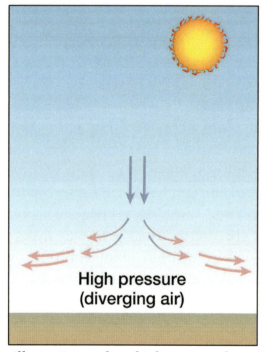

An illustration on how high pressure happens

Fun Facts

Why are clouds white if water is relatively clear?
While there might be other substances in the cloud, this isn't why they are white and visible. We see color because of how the sun's rays bounce off objects. It might sound weird, but a green object isn't actually green. It's actually every other color, but the object is repelling the green energy from the sun, which makes it look green. Clouds are white because the particles are large enough to deflect the white energy from the sun, which creates a distorted white color.

White clouds

Why are clouds black before a storm? There are several different reasons for this, but there's one prevalent reason. The cloud becomes super saturated with water molecules before it starts to rain due to the heating and cooling process that makes a storm happen. This makes the cloud thicker, which makes it harder for the sun's light to pass through it. This makes it look so dark.

Dark clouds

Clouds: Shapes, Forecasting and Fun Trivia about Clouds

Clouds are nothing more than the dense collection of billions of water droplets that have evaporated and collected into a clump. They stay together due to the intense cooling that happens high in the atmosphere, and because they are clinging to particles in the air like dust.

While most people call rain precipitation, this term can also be applied to snow, sleet and hail since they all fall from clouds. They just fall due to different reasons and environmental conditions.

Cody Miller

The vast majority of clouds are formed in the troposphere, which is the lowest part of our atmosphere. However, they can also be found higher in our atmosphere, such as in the stratosphere or mesosphere.

How much water do you think a cloud holds? The common cloud is formed from millions of tons of water. This is why they can cause so much rain and not disappear after a major storm.

Clouds: Shapes, Forecasting and Fun Trivia about Clouds

Fog is caused by a cloud coming too close to the ground, which is why it's so hard to see and why the air feels so different. You are looking through a lot of water vapor. This is commonly caused by stratus clouds that become too cool, which causes them to descend, but there are various reasons why this might happen. The thicker the fog, the closer the cloud is to the ground.

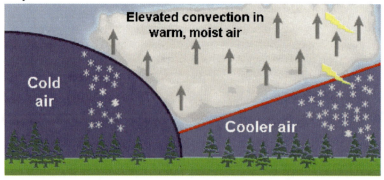

Clouds are most commonly formed from water, but they can also be made from chemicals. For example, if there's a chemical spill or dumping area with just enough water or liquid, then the evaporated particles can go into the air and form a cloud. This is dangerous because the cloud can poison the atmosphere and cause lethal or dangerous rains if the cloud gathers enough water.

Speaking of chemical clouds, every planet in our solar system has clouds. For example, Venus has clouds that are formed from sulfur dioxide. This is a very dangerous chemical that is similar to sulfuric acid. It can also cause significant health problems. If you have ever heard of acid rain, then you should know that it's caused by an abundance of sulfur dioxide in the air.

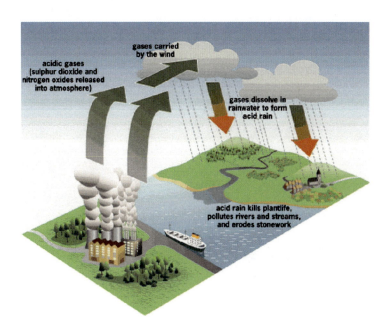

References

http://ellerbruch.nmu.edu/classes/cs255f02/cs255students/abarker/p4/clouds.html

http://www.nasa.gov/audience/forstudents/k-4/stories/what-are-clouds-k4.html

http://en.wikipedia.org/wiki/Cloud

http://blogs.channel4.com/liam-dutton-on-weather/clouds-form/4992

http://www.weatherwizkids.com/weather-clouds.htm

http://www.geography-site.co.uk/pages/physical/climate/why%20does%20it%20rain.html

http://www.sciencekids.co.nz/sciencefacts/weather/clouds.html

http://www.livescience.com/29436-clouds.html

http://johnb0127.hubpages.com/hub/The-Different-Types-of-Clouds

http://www.universetoday.com/41646/cumulonimbus-cloud/

http://www.woweather.com/reports/wxfacts/Nimbostratus.htm

http://www.wisegeek.com/what-is-stratocumulus.htm

http://www.instructables.com/id/Predicting-Weather-with-Clouds/?ALLSTEPS

http://www.mountwashington.org/education/center/arcade/cloud/folk.html

Gift For You

Go here for your gift:

http://freebiebonus.com/cloudaudiobookbonus

Made in the USA
Las Vegas, NV
05 January 2024

83972897R00024